THE OFFICIAL
RANGERS
ANNUAL 2016

Written by Roddy Mackenzie
Designed by Uta Dohlenburg

A Grange Publication

© 2015. Published by Grange Communications Ltd., Edinburgh, under licence from Rangers Football Club. Printed in the EU.

Photographs © Kirk O'Rourke, Rangers FC and Press Association Images

ISBN: 978-1-910199-53-4

CONTENTS

2014-15 SEASON REVIEW

AUGUST 5 – IBROX STADIUM: RANGERS 2 HIBERNIAN 1

Rangers opened the new season with an extra-time win over Hibs in the Petrofac Training Cup.
The home side made the perfect start, with Lewis Macleod scoring after just 13 minutes with a low shot.
Danny Handling equalised in the second half, but was later red-carded for a foul on David Templeton.
Rangers took full advantage with Nicky Law curling home the winner in extra-time.

AUGUST 10 – IBROX STADIUM: RANGERS 1 HEARTS 2

Rangers opened their league campaign in defeat as Hearts snatched an injury-time winner.
Current Ranger Danny Wilson gave Hearts the lead with a header, but Nicky Law thought he had salvaged a point for Rangers when he squeezed the ball home from close range in the last minute.
Osman Sow left the home side deflated, however, when he scored the winning goal with a precise finish in injury-time.

AUGUST 15 – FALKIRK STADIUM: FALKIRK 0 RANGERS 2

Rangers gathered their first league points of the season courtesy of late goals from Lewis Macleod and Nicky Clark. Both sides had chances, but the breakthrough didn't come until 13 minutes from time when Macleod's long-range effort broke off Will Vaulks to beat Jamie McDonald.
Rangers finished strongly, and Nicky Clark made sure of the points when he touched in a Nicky Law effort from close range.

AUGUST 18 – IBROX STADIUM: RANGERS 8 CLYDE 1

Rangers showed no mercy as former skipper Barry Ferguson brought his Clyde side to Ibrox to advance in the Petrofac Training Cup.
Kris Boyd celebrated his birthday with a well-taken hat-trick, as Rangers scored-at-will in a dominant display.
Rangers were 5-0 up at half-time through a Boyd double and strikes from Fraser Aird, Lee McCulloch and Lewis Macleod. Boyd, McCulloch and Macleod took it to 8-0 in the second half before Kevin Watt fired a last-minute consolation for Clyde.

AUGUST 23 – IBROX STADIUM: RANGERS 4 DUMBARTON 1

Rangers eased to three points after skipper Lee McCulloch set them on their way with a controlled volley after 15 minutes. Darren McGregor drilled home the second before half-time, and from that moment there was little doubt about the outcome.
Kris Boyd set up Nicky Clark for the third early in the second half, and then Chris Turner put the ball into his own net. Dumbarton pulled a goal back when Bilel Mohsni headed it past his own goalkeeper nine minutes from the end.

AUGUST 26 – NEW BROOMFIELD: QUEEN'S PARK 1 RANGERS 2

Rangers did not get things all their own way in Airdrie but did enough to secure their place in the second round of the League Cup.

Kris Boyd showed his predatory instincts with a fine double to set up a second-round place with Inverness Caledonian Thistle. He opened the scoring after just seven minutes and, after Tony Quinn had headed a 31st-minute equaliser, the striker headed what proved to be the winning goal into an empty net in 53 minutes.

AUGUST 30 – IBROX STADIUM: RANGERS 4 QUEEN OF THE SOUTH 2

Rangers had to come from behind to pick up another three league points against an enterprising Queen of the South.

Gavin Reilly beat Steve Simonsen to put Queens ahead midway through the first half, but Marius Zaliukas headed the equaliser. Iain Russell gave Queens a half-time lead, but substitute David Templeton turned the game with his contribution. He scored a stunning equaliser just after coming on, and Bilel Mohsni headed Rangers in front before Kenny Miller made sure of the points.

SEPTEMBER 2014

SEPTEMBER 12 – STARK'S PARK: RAITH ROVERS 0 RANGERS 4

Rangers moved to the top of the Championship with this convincing win. Again, Rangers had the points secured by half-time, with Nicky Clark, Ian Black and Nicky Law taking the game out of Raith's reach before the break. Lee McCulloch netted the final goal from the penalty spot after Lee Wallace had been brought down.

SEPTEMBER 16 – IBROX STADIUM: RANGERS 1 INVERNESS CT 0

Rangers claimed the scalp of a Premiership side to book their place in the third round of the League Cup.

Kris Boyd was denied by the Caley Thistle goalkeeper early on, but chances were few and far between in the tightest of contests. But Lewis Macleod gave Rangers a deserved win with a deflected shot with just 12 minutes left.

SEPTEMBER 20 – INDODRILL STADIUM: ALLOA ATHLETIC 1 RANGERS 1

It took a late goal from substitute David Templeton to secure a point for Rangers as Alloa proved difficult opponents.

Jonathan Tiffoney gave the home side the half-time lead with a 36th-minute header, and Rangers struggled to break down a well-organised Alloa defence. Templeton finally found the net, with eight minutes left, in a crowded penalty area to give Rangers a point.

SEPTEMBER 23 – FALKIRK STADIUM: FALKIRK 1 RANGERS 3

Rangers booked their place in the last eight of the League Cup after an early setback.
Former Ger Rory Loy gave Falkirk the lead inside five minutes, but Rangers equalised immediately when Owain Tudur Jones turned a cross into his own net. Dean Shiels put Rangers ahead in 65 minutes with a composed finish and Ian Black settled it with a long-range effort in the final moments.

SEPTEMBER 29 – IBROX STADIUM: RANGERS 1 HIBERNIAN 3

Rangers fell to their second league defeat after a painful first half.
After early Rangers pressure, Rangers fell behind to Jason Cummings' strike. David Gray headed a second before Cummings struck again six minutes from the break.
Nicky Law pulled a goal back with a terrific strike ten minutes into the second half but Hibs held on.

OCTOBER 2014

OCTOBER 4 – ENERGY ASSETS ARENA: LIVINGSTON 0 RANGERS 1

Rangers kept up the pursuit of pacesetters Hearts with a narrow win at Livingston. Lewis Macleod scored the only goal with a superb overhead kick after only eight minutes – a strike fit to win any game. Rangers tried to build on their lead, but some indifferent finishing meant they had to be content with just one goal.

OCTOBER 18 – IBROX STADIUM: RANGERS 6 RAITH ROVERS 1

Rangers rediscovered their scoring touch as they routed Raith at Ibrox.
Lee McCulloch set them on their way with a glancing header after eight minutes and Nicky Law added a second shortly before half-time.
Raith pulled a goal back through a Martin Scott header, but Rangers responded with Kenny Miller and Kris Boyd netting before a late brace from Jon Daly.

OCTOBER 21 – NEW BAYVIEW: EAST FIFE 0 RANGERS 2

Rangers reached the semi-finals of the Petrofac Training Cup with a comfortable win. Jon Daly broke the deadlock with a 29th-minute goal from point-blank range, no more than Rangers deserved in a disciplined first half. Ian Black effectively took the tie out of East Fife's reach with a 60th-minute free-kick.

OCTOBER 25 – BET BUTLER STADIUM: DUMBARTON 0 RANGERS 3

Rangers won with room to spare. Lee McCulloch saw a first-half penalty saved by Danny Rodgers but it didn't knock Rangers out of their stride.
Kenny Miller put Rangers in front shortly afterwards and then set up the second for Lee Wallace in the second half. Kris Boyd headed the third to underline Rangers' superiority.

OCTOBER 28 – IBROX STADIUM: RANGERS 1 ST JOHNSTONE 0

Rangers knocked out Premiership opposition for the second time to advance to the last four of the League Cup.
Lewis Macleod was the matchwinner, with a magnificent header with just four minutes left to stun the Perth side.
Ian Black and Kenny Miller almost added to Rangers' lead in the closing minutes as the home side finished on top.

NOVEMBER 2014

NOVEMBER 1 – BET BUTLER STADIUM: DUMBARTON 0 RANGERS 1

Kris Boyd proved the difference as Rangers booked their place in the fourth round of the Scottish Cup. The striker scored the only goal of the game – his eighth of the season – with a crisp finish on the stroke of half-time. Dumbarton made life difficult for Rangers, but the Ibrox men did enough to get through.

NOVEMBER 4 – CENTRAL PARK: COWDENBEATH 0 RANGERS 3

Rangers stretched their unbeaten run to seven matches with a comfortable victory. Nicky Law opened the scoring with a low shot after just three minutes, and Kyle Miller then headed into his own net to double Rangers' advantage. David Templeton came off the bench to slide home the third goal late on.

NOVEMBER 8 – IBROX STADIUM: RANGERS 4 FALKIRK 0

Rangers beat Falkirk for the third time this season, but it took time for them to stamp their superiority on the game.

Nicky Law put Rangers ahead after a mistake by Luke Leahy to give the home side a slender half-time lead.

Lewis Macleod headed in a Jon Daly cross to make it 2-0, then set up Kenny Miller for the third. Nicky Clark prodded home the final goal.

NOVEMBER 15 – IBROX STADIUM: RANGERS 1 ALLOA 1

Rangers dropped two points in the Championship title race on a frustrating day. Lee McCulloch looked to have set Rangers on the path to victory when he put the home side in front after 72 minutes. But six minutes later, Alloa scored a shock equaliser when Liam Buchanan found the roof of the net after Steve Simonsen had produced an excellent one-handed save to keep out Kevin Cawley's initial attempt.

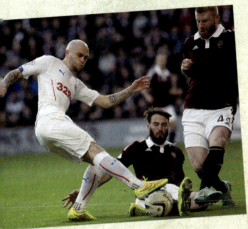

NOVEMBER 22 – TYNECASTLE PARK: HEARTS 2 RANGERS 0

Hearts claimed an important three points in the title race when Rangers were reduced to ten men after 20 minutes as Steven Smith was sent off for a foul on Callum Paterson. Hearts took full advantage and Jason Holt put them in front with a fine strike after 55 minutes.

Jamie Walker drilled home the second from the penalty spot with three minutes left, as Hearts moved further clear at the top.

NOVEMBER 30 – IBROX STADIUM: RANGERS 3 KILMARNOCK 0

Rangers added their third top-flight scalp of the season to reach the fifth round of the Scottish Cup. Nicky Law opened the scoring with a soaring 20-yard strike in the 19th minute. Substitute Kris Boyd made it 2-0 with 20 minutes left, netting against his former club, while Law thumped home a memorable third goal seven minutes from time.

DECEMBER 2014

DECEMBER 3 – INDODRILL STADIUM: ALLOA ATHLETIC 3 RANGERS 2

Rangers went out of the Petrofac Training Cup at the semi-final stage after controlling much of the tie at Alloa. The Ibrox men looked to be coasting into the final when Kenny Miller put them ahead early in the second half and Dean Shiels added a second in 64 minutes. But two goals in five minutes from Greig Spence and Ryan McCord turned the tie on its head. Spence scored his second goal with just a minute left, side-footing home from close range to put Alloa into the final.

DECEMBER 6 – IBROX STADIUM: RANGERS 1 COWDENBEATH 0

Rangers did not fire on all cylinders but did enough to collect all three points against a stubborn Cowdenbeath side. Dean Shiels – with his third goal of the campaign – settled it after 58 minutes when he stroked the ball past Robbie Thomson after good work from Kenny Miller.

DECEMBER 12 – PALMERSTON PARK: QUEEN OF THE SOUTH 2 RANGERS 0

Queen of the South laid down their title credentials with a win at Palmerston that moved them to within four points of Rangers. The home side played some enterprising football, and they were rewarded when Kevin Holt gave them a half-time lead. Zander Clark produced some great saves to keep Rangers at bay, before Gavin Reilly rifled home an unstoppable second goal.

DECEMBER 20 – IBROX STADIUM: RANGERS 2 LIVINGSTON 0

Rangers got their title challenge back on track by beating Livingston. Fraser Aird set them on their way with a goal after only 10 minutes with a great strike. Rangers had to be patient as Livingston tried to hit back, but the points were secure after 73 minutes when Simon Mensing headed an Aird cross into his own net.

DECEMBER 27 – EASTER ROAD STADIUM: HIBERNIAN 4 RANGERS 0

Caretaker-manager Kenny McDowall saw his side slip to a disappointing defeat.
Hibs scored twice in the opening 12 minutes – David Gray scoring with a wonderful strike and Jason Cummings added a second. Scott Robertson ensured there was no way back for Rangers, with a third goal midway through the second half and Liam Craig later added a fourth.

JANUARY 2015

JANUARY 3 – IBROX STADIUM: RANGERS 3 DUMBARTON 1

Rangers opened the new year by collecting three points after falling behind to an early strike from Andy Graham. But Jon Daly equalised midway through the first half, and Lee Wallace put Rangers in front with a precise finish four minutes before half time. Rangers were not sure of the points until Dean Shiels netted a third goal in the final minute.

JANUARY 10 – INDODRILL STADIUM: ALLOA ATHLETIC 0 RANGERS 1

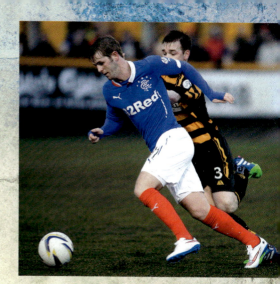

Rangers had failed to beat Alloa in three attempts and were grateful for three points thanks to Nicky Law's tenth goal of the season. In difficult conditions, Law slid the ball home from close range after Jon Daly had cut the ball back after 15 minutes. Both teams had chances after this but the early strike was to prove sufficient for Rangers.

FEBRUARY 2015

FEBRUARY 1 – HAMPDEN PARK: CELTIC 2 RANGERS 0

Celtic took the honours in the first Old Firm clash for almost three years and clinched a place in the League Cup final. Leigh Griffiths headed Celtic in front and Kris Commons fired home a stunning second goal before half-time. Rangers fought for every ball, but could not make much impression on a well-organised Celtic rearguard.

FEBRUARY 8 – IBROX STADIUM: RANGERS 1 RAITH ROVERS 2

Raith ended Rangers' interest in the Scottish Cup with a shock win at Ibrox. Ryan Conroy put Raith in front with a well-taken free-kick, but Haris Vuckic equalised with a precise finish into the corner. Christian Nade scored what proved to be the winner after 75 minutes, when the ball broke to him a yard from goal. But Kris Boyd should have equalised with a header in the dying minutes.

FEBRUARY 13 – IBROX STADIUM: RANGERS 0 HIBERNIAN 2

Rangers suffered their third successive defeat as Hibs moved up to second in the Championship.
The home side started well, but Scott Robertson put Hibs ahead after hesitancy in the home defence.
Lewis Stevenson ensured the points were bound for Edinburgh when he scored Hibs' second after a volley with just nine minutes left.

FEBRUARY 20 – STARK'S PARK: RAITH ROVERS 1 RANGERS 2

Rangers snapped their three-game losing streak to gain revenge for their Scottish Cup exit.
Andy Murdoch scored a superb goal to put Rangers in front after 35 minutes and Kris Boyd scrambled home a second early in the second half to leave Raith in trouble.
Ryan Conroy pulled a goal back with a fine effort but Rangers had the points in the bag.

FEBRUARY 27 – FALKIRK STADIUM: FALKIRK 1 RANGERS 1

Rangers had to settle for a point in a tight encounter.
Darren McGregor thumped home the opener for
Rangers after 20 minutes, but Falkirk hit back.
Rory Loy looped in a header just two minutes later to
draw Falkirk level.
Neither side took a firm grip on the game after that and
a draw was a fair outcome.

MARCH 2015

MARCH 7 – CENTRAL PARK: COWDENBEATH 0 RANGERS 0

Rangers drew a blank at Central Park on a barren afternoon. Cowdenbeath were well organised at the back
and although Rangers dominated for long spells, they were restricted to a few opportunities.
Skipper Lee McCulloch came closest, with a near-post header in the first half that came back off the
crossbar.

MARCH 10 – IBROX STADIUM: RANGERS 1 QUEEN OF THE SOUTH 1

Queen of the South showed why they were challenging for a play-off place with a decent display.
Jon Daly missed a chance for Rangers in the first half, but Gavin Reilly hit woodwork at the other end.
Haris Vuckic looked to have won it for Rangers when he slid the ball home in 77 minutes, but substitute
Aidan Smith scored a late equaliser for Queens.

MARCH 14 – IBROX STADIUM: RANGERS 1 LIVINGSTON 1

Rangers were under the tenure of
Stuart McCall for the first time and
Haris Vuckic gave him the perfect start
with an early goal. Tom Walsh almost
marked his full debut with a goal, but
it was Livingston who found the net
through Ibra Sekajja on the stroke of
half-time.
Kenny Miller thought he had won it
for Rangers in the closing minutes
with a header, but Darren Jamieson
pulled off an unbelievable save.

MARCH 17 – IBROX STADIUM: RANGERS 2 ALLOA ATHLETIC 2

Rangers endured their fifth successive draw as Alloa frustrated them again at Ibrox. A glancing header from Ben Gordon early in the second half gave Alloa the lead against the run of play, but Nicky Clark turned the tables with a well-taken double. But there was a sting in the tale for Rangers when Liam Buchanan equalised after eluding the home defence to clip the ball home in 81 minutes.

MARCH 22 – EASTER ROAD STADIUM: HIBERNIAN 0 RANGERS 2

Rangers returned to winning ways to close the gap on Hibs and boost their play-off hopes.
Lee Wallace broke the deadlock two minutes from half-time when he swept the ball home after a scramble in the penalty area. Kenny Miller made sure of victory when he ran at the Hibs defence and tucked the ball behind Mark Oxley to settle the issue.

MARCH 28 – IBROX STADIUM: RANGERS 4 COWDENBEATH 1

Rangers had all the pressure in the first half but were kept out by Robbie Thomson in the Cowdenbeath goal. Nicky Clark opened the scoring just after the break when he bundled the ball in from close range. Cowdenbeath equalised through Kudus Oyenuga but Darren McGregor cracked home Rangers' second from outside the area. Haris Vuckic added two neatly-taken goals to underline Rangers' superiority.

APRIL 2015

APRIL 5 – IBROX STADIUM: RANGERS 2 HEARTS 1

Rangers produced arguably their best display of the season to beat the champions at Ibrox. Lee Wallace fed Kenny Miller for the opener after 28 minutes and Haris Vuckic scored a brilliant second goal from the edge of the area. Lee McCulloch was sent off before half-time for using an elbow, to leave Rangers with much work to do. But they held on for the three points as Genero Zeefuik pulled a goal back eight minutes from time.

APRIL 9 – PALMERSTON PARK: QUEEN OF THE SOUTH 3 RANGERS 0

Rangers' hopes of moving back into second place in the Championship were dashed by a lethal Queens.

Derek Lyle gave the home side a half-time lead with a crisply-struck shot in 33 minutes. It was 2-0 just after half-time when Lewis Kidd put the ball back across goal and it came off Lee Wallace and into the net. Gavin Reilly made it 3-0 after beating the offside trap as Rangers chased the game.

APRIL 12 – IBROX STADIUM: RANGERS 4 RAITH ROVERS 0

Rangers needed three points to maintain their challenge and Nicky Clark headed them in front from a corner. Haris Vuckic then scored a wonderful second goal when he drilled the ball into the far corner from the edge of the area. Nicky Law added a third after his initial shot had come back off the crossbar and he then added the fourth with an inventive strike from 18 yards.

APRIL 15 – ENERGY ASSETS ARENA: LIVINGSTON 1 RANGERS 1

Rangers moved second in the Championship but had to settle for just a point against a battling Livingston. Miles Hippolyte put Livingston in front with a curling free-kick early in the second half, but Rangers hit back immediately when Marius Zaliukas struck. Haris Vuckic struck the post as Rangers pressed for victory but Livingston held out.

APRIL 18 – BET BUTLER STADIUM: DUMBARTON 1 RANGERS 3

It was a case of Ryan Hardie at the double as Rangers picked up another three points at Dumbarton. But it was Dumbarton who drew first blood after just two minutes when Mark Wilson sent the ball beyond Cammy Bell. Hardie bundled in the equaliser after being sent clear by Haris Vuckic, and then netted his second after the break. Vuckic curled home a stunning third goal for Rangers – his eighth since joining the club.

APRIL 25 – IBROX STADIUM: RANGERS 2 FALKIRK 2

Rangers stormed back from two goals down to earn a point but the result saw them drop to third in the league with just one game of the regular season left. After a goalless first half, John Baird scored from close range. Tom Taiwo then made it 2-0 after 61 minutes. But Rangers came back, and Haris Vuckic pulled a goal back when he headed home a corner in 81 minutes. Nicky Law then equalised in injury-time with a low shot for a hard-earned point.

MAY 2015

MAY 2 – TYNECASTLE STADIUM: HEARTS 2 RANGERS 2

Rangers had to settle for third place in the Championship as the champions refused to accept defeat. Darren McGregor headed Rangers in front after 32 minutes, and Kenny Miller swept home the second goal before the break to put the champions in deep trouble. But Hearts displayed the character they had shown all season to power back and earn a point. Genero Zeefuik pulled a goal back after 81 minutes with a header, then equalised in the final minute.

MAY 9 – PALMERSTON PARK: QUEEN OF THE SOUTH 1 RANGERS 2

Rangers claimed a crucial advantage in the first leg of their play-off in Dumfries.

Steven Smith eased Rangers' nerves with a well-struck free-kick just before half-time before Derek Lyle equalised for the home side with a second-half header. But Dean Shiels headed home Richard Foster's cross with 15 minutes left to settle the first leg encounter, his first goal since December.

MAY 17 – IBROX STADIUM: RANGERS 1 QUEEN OF THE SOUTH 1

Rangers did enough to qualify for a semi-final showdown with Hibernian in a tense tie at Ibrox.
Derek Lyle shocked Ibrox when he headed Queens in front after 35 minutes to level the scores on aggregate before Lee Wallace equalised with half-an-hour left. But the drama wasn't over as Haris Vuckic made a superb clearance on the line to prevent Lyle taking the tie to extra-time.

MAY 20 – IBROX STADIUM: RANGERS 2 HIBERNIAN 0

Rangers put one foot in the play-off final by putting Hibs to the sword.
Nicky Clark scored the vital opening goal after great work from Richard Foster just a minute from the break.
Kenny Miller then doubled Rangers' advantage when he scored against his former club after 61 minutes.

MAY 23 – EASTER ROAD STADIUM: HIBERNIAN 1 RANGERS 0

It was mission accomplished for Rangers as they secured their berth in the play-off final.
Hibs had plenty of possession but not much penetration, and Rangers comfortably dealt with most of what they could muster. The only goal – deep into injury-time from Jason Cummings – came too late for the home side.

MAY 28 – IBROX STADIUM: RANGERS 1 MOTHERWELL 3

Motherwell withstood some early pressure and then hit Rangers with a sucker-punch just before half-time.
Lee Erwin squeezed home the opener after 27 minutes and Stephen McManus then headed home a second.
Lionel Ainsworth made it 3-0 shortly after the break, before a late goal from Darren McGregor gave Rangers some hope of salvaging things in the second leg.

MAY 31 – FIR PARK: MOTHERWELL 3 RANGERS 0

Rangers' fate was sealed as Motherwell conjured up the goals that mattered in a match that turned ugly.
After a goalless first half, Marvin Johnson broke the deadlock with a deflected effort that caught out Cammy Bell. Lionel Ainsworth made it 2-0 with the help of another deflection and John Sutton completed the scoring from the penalty spot. The match had a shameful ending with Rangers' substitute Bilel Mohsni, Motherwell's Lee Erwin and unused substitute Fraser Kerr all red-carded.

RANGERS A to Z

A is for **Advocaat** – Dutchman Dick enjoyed a trophy-laden time as manager.

B is for **Barcelona** – the scene of Rangers' only European triumph in 1972.

C is for **Callander** – Rangers' first opponents in May 1872, the match ended goalless.

D is for **Davie** – Wing-king Cooper was simply one of the best.

E is for **European Golden Boot** – record goalscorer Ally McCoist twice won the award for Europe's top scorer.

F is for **Fans** – Rangers have supporters' clubs all over the world who give the club fantastic backing.

G is for "**Gazza**" – Paul Gascoigne enjoyed a special bond with the Rangers' fans.

H is for **Helicopter** – who can forget the day the helicopter changed direction with the SPL trophy on the final day of the 2004-05 season.

I is for **Ibrox** – the stadium has been Rangers' home since 1899.

is for **Jardine** – Sandy made a huge contribution to the club as a player and as an ambassador.

is for **Kelvinside** – Rangers' joint-record victory was 13-0 against these opponents in the Scottish Cup in 1889.

is for **Laudrup** – Great Dane Brian thrilled the Ibrox crowd with his talents.

is for **Murray Park** – the training ground is the assembly-line for Rangers' stars of the future.

is for **Nine** – The number of league titles Rangers won in succession under Graeme Souness and Walter Smith.

is for **Old Firm** – the greatest rivalry in world football.

is for **President** – Rangers' greatest-ever player John Greig was named honorary life president of the club in May 2015.

is for **Queen's Park** – Rangers first played their Glasgow rivals in a competitive match back in 1879 in a Scottish Cup tie.

is for **Ready** – the Rangers' motto.

is for **Struth** – legend Bill is the most successful manager in the club's history

is for **Treble** – Rangers have won the domestic treble on no fewer than seven occasions, a world record.

is for **UEFA Cup** – Rangers reached the final of the 2007-08 version in Manchester.

is for **Vale of Leven** – Rangers reached their first Scottish Cup final in 1877 against Vale.

is for **Walter** – Smith's two spells as manager had a silver lining.

is for **X-ray** – never a good sign for a Rangers player as, more often than not, it means serious injury.

is for **Young** – defender George played almost 300 games for Rangers between 1941-57 and won 54 Scotland caps.

is for **Zenit St Petersburg** – Rangers' opponents, managed by Dick Advocaat, in the 2008 UEFA Cup final.

CAMMY BELL

DATE OF BIRTH:
18.09.86
POSITION:
GOALKEEPER

The experienced goalkeeper made his name at Kilmarnock, spending nine years at Rugby Park including loan spells at Montrose and Queen of the South.

He won a League Cup winners' medal with the Ayrshire club in 2012 when he was voted Man of the Match after the final win over Celtic.

Cammy gained a full Scotland cap in a win over the Faroes in 2010 and arrived at Ibrox in the summer of 2013.

WES FODERINGHAM

DATE OF BIRTH:
14.01.91
POSITION:
GOALKEEPER

Foderingham represented England at youth level, and joined Rangers in the summer after becoming a free agent since leaving Swindon Town.

The goalkeeper spent four years at Swindon, making over 150 appearances, the club winning the League Two title in his first season. He started out with Fulham but signed his first pro contract with Crystal Palace in 2010.

LIAM KELLY

DATE OF BIRTH:
30.01.96
POSITION:
GOALKEEPER

Liam has come up through the youth ranks at Ibrox and has impressed with his commanding displays for club and country.

Capped for Scotland at Under-16, Under-17 and Under-19 level, he signed a new two-and-a-half year deal with the club early in 2015 that ties him to the club until 2018.

ROB KIERNAN

DATE OF BIRTH:
13.01.91
POSITION:
DEFENDER

The much-travelled defender started out with Watford and captained their Under-18 team. He was given his full debut by then-manager Brendan Rodgers and went on to captain the Republic of Ireland at Under-19 and Under-21 levels.

Including loan spells, Kiernan played for 11 clubs before signing for Rangers last summer. This includes a spell at Kilmarnock under Jimmy Calderwood, making his debut in a 1-0 win over Celtic.

JAMES TAVERNIER

DATE OF BIRTH:
31.10.91
POSITION:
DEFENDER

Tavernier joined the club on a three-year contract from Wigan Athletic in the summer after spending the latter part of last season on loan at Bristol City.

He played a key role in the team, winning the League One title, and will look to add more honours with Rangers.

He started out with Leeds United as a youth before joining Newcastle United where he spent six years, but only made two first-team appearances. Tavernier made his breakthrough with Rotherham United, helping them to promotion to the Championship in 2014 before signing for Wigan.

LEE WALLACE

DATE OF BIRTH:
01.08.87
POSITION:
DEFENDER

Lee was a fans-favourite at Hearts where he spent seven years before joining Rangers in 2011. The 28 year-old full back, who just loves to get forward quickly, won over the Ibrox faithful with his adventurous style.

He played for Scotland at Under-19 and Under-21 level before making his full Scotland debut in a friendly match against Japan. Lee was the club's Player of the Year in 2014 and also the Players' Player of the Year.

DOMINIC BALL

DATE OF BIRTH:
02.08.95
POSITION:
DEFENDER

Dominic came through the youth system at Tottenham Hotspur and can play as a defensive midfield player or in central defence. He signed a season-long loan deal at Ibrox last August.

Loaned out to Cambridge United until the end of last season, he made his professional debut in a 1-1 draw with Dagenham and Redbridge in January 2015.

After playing for Northern Ireland at youth level, he switched his allegiance to England in 2013 and has been capped for his country of birth at Under-20 level.

DANNY WILSON

DATE OF BIRTH:
27.12.91
POSITION:
DEFENDER

The former Rangers' Under-19 captain returned to Ibrox last summer after helping Hearts win the Championship.

The highly-rated defender played for Rangers in the Champions League at the age of 17, and has been capped by Scotland at Under-17, Under-19, Under-21 and full level. He scored on his full international debut against the Faroes in a 3-0 friendly win.

Danny signed for Liverpool in 2010 before being loaned out to Blackpool, Bristol City and Hearts, before signing for the Tynecastle side on a full-time basis.

NICKY LAW

DATE OF BIRTH:
29.03.88
POSITION:
MIDFIELDER

The Plymouth-born midfielder started his career with Sheffield United, but didn't enjoy an extended run in the first-team and was loaned out to Yeovil Town and Bradford City.

He signed for Rotherham in 2009, then moved north of the Border to sign for Stuart McCall's Motherwell two years later, making his debut against Inverness Caledonian Thistle. Rangers snapped him up on a free transfer in May, 2013.

ANDY HALLIDAY

DATE OF BIRTH:
11.10.91
POSITION:
MIDFIELDER

Andy joined the club in the summer after leaving Bradford City at the end of last season.

He scored a memorable goal in Bradford's historic win over Chelsea at Stamford Bridge in the FA Cup last season.

Starting out at Livingston, he was signed by Gordon Strachan for Middlesbrough and spent four years there before moving to Bradford.

NATHAN ODUWA

DATE OF BIRTH:
05.03.96
POSITION:
MIDFIELDER

The Londoner moved north on a season-long loan deal from Tottenham Hotspur with Dominic Ball last summer.

Nathan made his debut as a substitute against Alloa Athletic where he immediately caught the eye with his skills.

An attacking midfielder with an eye for goal, he was on loan with Luton Town in League Two last season where he played 11 matches. He was capped by England at Under-17 and Under-18 level.

FRASER AIRD

DATE OF BIRTH:
02.02.95
POSITION:
MIDFIELDER

Born in Toronto to Scottish parents, Fraser signed for his boyhood heroes at the age of 16. The winger quickly progressed through the youth ranks and was recognised at international level, with Scotland capping him at Under-17 and Under-19 level.

He broke into the first-team in the 2012-13 season under Ally McCoist and quickly established himself as a regular in the team.

GEDION ZELALEM

DATE OF BIRTH:
26.01.97
POSITION:
MIDFIELDER

The teenager made his debut in a 5-0 win over Airdrieonians in August.

The Berlin-born midfield player has played for Germany at Under-17 level, but has since switched allegiance to the USA and played for them at the Under-20 World Cup last May where the Americans reached the quarter-finals.

After playing for Arsenal at youth level, he made his debut for the Gunners when he came off the bench for the final 20 minutes of an FA Cup tie against Coventry City last January.

DEAN SHIELS

DATE OF BIRTH:
01.02.85
POSITION:
MIDFIELDER

The Northern Ireland international started out with Arsenal as a youth, but came to prominence after signing for Hibernian in 2004. He played over 100 games for the Edinburgh club before moving south to Doncaster Rovers.

Dean returned to play for Kilmarnock, initially on loan, then signed for Rangers where he has provided a decent supply of goals.

JASON HOLT

DATE OF BIRTH:
19.02.93
POSITION:
MIDFIELDER

The midfield player signed for Hearts from an early age and it didn't take him long to make an impact for the first team.

Holt scored goals against both halves of the Old Firm before joining Sheffield United last January. There he scored five goals in 11 matches before his loan spell came to an end.

A player who relishes the big occasion, he has been capped for Scotland at Under-21 level.

JORDAN THOMPSON

DATE OF BIRTH:
03.01.97
POSITION:
MIDFIELDER

The Belfast-born midfielder signed a two-year deal with the club in the summer. Thompson previously played for Manchester United where he spent four years at their academy. A lifelong Rangers fan, he impressed in a trial game against Tottenham and was offered terms.

DAVID TEMPLETON

DATE OF BIRTH:
07.01.89
POSITION:
MIDFIELDER

David attracted a lot of interest when he played for Stenhousemuir as a youngster, and it was Hearts who gave him the chance to play at the top level in Scotland. A scorer of spectacular goals, he can light up a game with flashes of genius. One of the highlights of his career so far is scoring for Hearts against Liverpool at Anfield in the Europa League in 2012, his final goal for the club before joining Rangers.

TOM WALSH

DATE OF BIRTH:
11.07.96
POSITION:
MIDFIELDER

A Scotland youth cap, the talented player made his Rangers debut at the age of just 16 when he came on as a substitute in a match against Stirling Albion in December 2012.

The teenager has had injury worries to contend with, but Tom has never let the team down when called into action.

BARRIE McKAY

DATE OF BIRTH:
30.12.94
POSITION:
MIDFIELDER

The wide player joined the club from Kilmarnock in 2011 and is living up to his potential after joining the first-team squad at Ibrox the following season.

He signed a five-year contract for the club back in 2012, he's proved he can create chances for others but has also shown he has an eye for goal.

A Scotland Under-21 cap, McKay is keen to cement a long-term future at Ibrox.

KENNY MILLER

DATE OF BIRTH:
23.12.79
POSITION:
STRIKER

In his third spell at the club, the Scotland international striker still knows the way to the goal, as he proved last season. A tireless worker, Kenny never gives less than 100 per cent.

Capped 69 times for his country and having scored 18 international goals, his talents have graced many other clubs as well as Rangers, namely, Hibs, Wolves, Celtic, Derby County, Bursaspor, Cardiff City and Vancouver Whitecaps.

MARTYN WAGHORN

DATE OF BIRTH:
23.01.90
POSITION:
STRIKER

Another of Mark Warburton's summer signings, Waghorn made his Sunderland debut at the age of just 17 in 2007 against Manchester United.

He had loan spells at Charlton Athletic and Leicester City before he signed a permanent deal with the latter club in a £3million transfer in 2010.

Waghorn had further loan spells at Hull City and Millwall before signing for Wigan Athletic. He was capped twice by England at Under-21 level, scoring in both matches.

RYAN HARDIE

DATE OF BIRTH:
17.03.97
POSITION:
STRIKER

Ryan made his first appearance for the club when he came on as a late substitute in a League Cup match against Falkirk last season. He had to wait a few months for his first league game, again coming off the bench, but he made his mark in a match at Dumbarton last April when he scored twice – his first goals for the club.

NICKY CLARK

DATE OF BIRTH:
03.06.91
POSITION:
STRIKER

The son of former Rangers striker Sandy, Nicky knows all about finding the net. He had a remarkable final season at Queen of the South in 2012-13 where he scored 41 goals, prompting Ally McCoist to bring him to Ibrox.

An injury early in his time at Ibrox held him back, but now he is out to make up for lost time by consistently banging in the goals.

Rangers have been blessed with some world-class goalkeepers through the years. Here, we look at some of the best.

SAFE

Jerry Dawson (1929-1945)

Dawson signed professional terms with Rangers in 1929 and went on to enjoy 16 happy years at Ibrox.

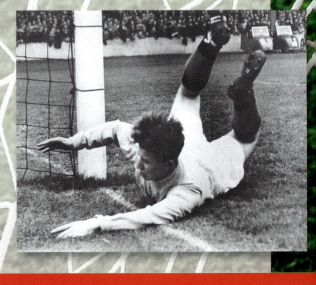

He played 236 league games for the club and helped Rangers to five league titles during his time between the sticks. He also celebrated two Scottish Cup triumphs with the club.

He was capped 14 times for Scotland, went on to play for Falkirk and later managed East Fife to the League Cup. He died in 1977 at the age of 67.

George Niven (1951-1960)

Signed by legendary manager Bill Struth in 1951, he spent over ten years at Ibrox and made 327 appearances in total.

He won five league championship medals, as well as helping the team to two Scottish Cups and one League Cup.

Niven was capped by the Scottish League, but never won a full international cap. He was twice selected but had to withdraw on both occasions due to injury. He died at the age of 79 in 2008.

HANDS

Peter McCloy (1970-1986)

McCloy signed for Rangers from Motherwell in 1970 and for most of the next 16 years he was first-choice goalkeeper at Ibrox.

"The Girvan Lighthouse" played more times for Rangers (535) than any other goalkeeper and was in the team that won the European Cup-Winners' Cup in 1972, beating Moscow Dynamo in the final in Barcelona. Capped on four occasions by Scotland, he played under three different managers at Ibrox (Willie Waddell, Jock Wallace and John Greig) and won two league titles, four Scottish Cups and four League Cups. He retired as a player in 1986.

Chris Woods (1986-1991)

The England international goalkeeper arrived at Rangers as part of the Graeme Souness revolution in 1986 in a £600,000 move from Norwich City.

He won the league championship and League Cup in his first season, and from November 1986 to January 1987 he set a British record of

playing for 1,196 minutes without conceding a goal.
Capped 43 times by England, he played 230 competitive matches for Rangers and won the Scottish League in four of his five seasons before leaving to join Sheffield Wednesday in 1991 for £1.2 million.

Andy Goram (1991-1998)

Goram succeeded Woods at Ibrox after signing in a £1 million deal from Hibernian in 1991 and soon won over the Ibrox faithful.

He enjoyed a league and Scottish Cup double in his first season and became a mainstay in the team for the next seven years, making 260 appearances and going on to win 43 Scotland caps.

The following season he was even more successful, winning the domestic treble and playing a big part in Rangers almost getting to the final of the revamped Champions League. He was voted Scottish Player of the Year.

Rangers' fans voted him best-ever Rangers goalkeeper in a poll in 1999.

Stefan Klos (1998-2007)

There was no doubting the credentials of Stefan Klos, the German arriving at Ibrox as a Champions League winner with Borussia Dortmund the previous year.

He won a championship medal in his first season with the club and, in 2002-2003, he helped the team win the domestic treble. Klos became the first goalkeeper to be named Rangers' captain in the summer of 2004.

In all, he played 298 games for the club and won four Scottish League titles, three Scottish Cups and two League Cups. He retired at the age of 36.

Allan McGregor (2001-2012)

Edinburgh-born McGregor came through the youth ranks at Ibrox and went on to play 278 matches for the club, as well as having loan spells at St Johnstone and Dunfermline Athletic.

He became a first-team regular at the start of the 2006-07 season and went on to win three league titles, three Scottish Cups and five League Cups before departing for Turkish side Besiktas in 2012, although he missed Rangers' UEFA Cup final appearance in 2008 due to injury.

He made his international debut for Scotland against Austria in 2007 and has gone on to play more than 30 games for his country.

FUTURE FORCE

Rangers' Under-20 team finished fourth in the Scottish Development League in 2014-15. Here, we look back on some of the highlights from the season.

NOVEMBER 26, 2014
RANGERS 4 DUNDEE UNITED 1

Andy Murdoch bagged a double as Rangers saw off Dundee United in the Scottish Development League. Murdoch opened the scoring in the first half, but Dundee United hit back to level the game.

Rangers secured a half-time lead when Nicky Clark's header beat the United goalkeeper with the aid of a deflection.

The home side drove home their advantage in the second period with Fraser Aird scoring with a free-kick and Murdoch grabbing his second goal of the match to kill off United.

FEBRUARY 3, 2015
RANGERS 5 HEARTS 1

Hearts included seven first-team squad players in their starting eleven, but Rangers put them to the sword with a stirring first-half display at Murray Park in the Scottish Development League.

Rangers included Lee Robinson, Marius Zaliukas and David Templeton from the first-team in their starting line-up, but it was Hearts who took an early lead when Brad McKay scored from the penalty spot.

Calum Gallagher had a penalty saved before Templeton equalised with a terrific strike. Zaliukas headed Rangers in front, before Tom Walsh made it 3-1 from the penalty spot and Ryan Hardie scored a fourth before half-time. Walsh collected his second goal after the break as Rangers coasted to all three points.

FEBRUARY 23, 2015
RANGERS 0 ST JOHNSTONE 0 (RANGERS WIN 3-2 ON PENALTIES)

Rangers squeezed into the semi-finals of the SFA Youth Cup after a dramatic penalty shoot-out at Ibrox. The teams could not be separated after 120 minutes of football and Rangers held their nerve to win it.

It was a tight affair throughout, with the respective goalkeepers Liam Kelly and Mark Hurst handling everything that came their way.

Chances were few and far between in normal time, but Kyle Lander had an opportunity to give St Johnstone the lead midway through the second half, only to be denied by Kelly.

Rangers squandered a handful of chances in normal time and in the extra period, but it all came right in the penalty shoot-out. Tom Walsh, Fraser Aird and Ryan Hardie were all on target, and Lander and Jason Kerr scored for Saints. But it was Kelly who was the hero with saves from Connor McLaren and Paul Esslemont.

MARCH 12, 2015
RANGERS 6 ROSS COUNTY 1

Ryan Hardie made light of atrocious conditions at Murray Park to fire home a hat-trick in the Scottish Development League.

He scored his first after just seven minutes when he headed home a cross from Fraser Aird, and ten minutes later Calum Gallagher added a second with a controlled finish.

Hardie made it 3-0 three minutes later when he showed great composure to score, and Darren Ramsay added the fourth with an angled drive ten minutes from the break.

Hardie completed his hat-trick in the second half and Gallagher grabbed his second as County wilted, although they did manage a consolation goal.

MAY 3, 2015
RANGERS 1 AYR UNITED 0

Rangers reached the final of the SFA Youth Cup for the second year in a row with a narrow victory at Ibrox. The home side should have won by a greater margin

SCOTTISH DEVELOPMENT LEAGUE TABLE 2014-15

	P	W	D	L	GF	GA	GD	PTS
Aberdeen	32	25	2	5	87	37	50	77
Celtic	32	21	6	5	70	31	39	69
Hamilton	32	20	2	10	78	42	36	62
Rangers	32	17	6	9	67	46	21	57
Hibernian	32	13	12	7	75	54	21	51
Falkirk	32	15	6	11	46	46	0	51
Partick Th	32	14	4	14	58	72	-14	46
Motherwell	32	13	6	13	61	50	11	45
St Johnstone	32	12	6	14	40	46	-6	42
Dundee Utd	32	12	4	16	57	60	-3	40
Dundee	32	12	4	16	40	57	-17	40
Kilmarnock	32	11	6	15	49	59	-10	39
St Mirren	32	10	9	13	44	54	-10	39
Dunfermline	32	10	3	19	52	59	-7	33
Hearts	32	8	3	21	46	78	-32	27
Ross County	32	4	13	15	54	82	-28	25
Inverness CT	32	5	8	19	33	84	-51	23

but Ayr goalkeeper Shaun Newman had an inspired game between the sticks.

Ryan Hardie hit the crossbar early on and Rangers had numerous chances in the first half, but the killer touch deserted them in front of goal.

The only goal of the game came in 57 minutes when Hardie set up Fraser Aird and his shot beat Newman with the aid of a deflection.

Hardie could have made things more comfortable for Rangers in the closing stages but was twice thwarted by excellent saves from Newman. It set up a final clash with Celtic, which Rangers lost 5-2.

Can you find 20 Rangers greats in our Wordsearch?

You can go **horizontally, vertically, diagonally** and **backwards.**

```
M W G L F X T G W M G N Q F K
H C X T F F R I G A K V Q K Q
G G K Q H W L G S N K Q O H K
O P U R B K G C B H K S T G B
R U T O I E O R A J U Y N Z K
A R V N G I N T E R K F R R D
M D S B G K E A O I Y K E K T
R U L N R L R M L O G T P R S
J A E N E A A D L R X P O C I
A L Q Y L J N C W A A K O T O
R N I E T S C D B M T P C Q C
D R H Z R M B B U T C H E R C
I Q F R L N L R O G E R G C M
N H E N D E R S O N T M Z Y K
E Y B H G U O L L I W C L Q T
```

McCoist	Gascoigne	Henderson	Gough
McCloy	Willoughby	Greig	Wilkins
Butcher	Parlane	Goram	McGregor
Brand	Laudrup	Hateley	Cooper
Jardine	Baxter	Stein	Amoruso

WORDSEARCH

QUIZ

**Take a look back to the 2014-15 Season.
How much do you remember?**

1. Who scored Rangers' first competitive goal of the season in early August?
2. Who scored Rangers' first league goal of the campaign?
3. What was Rangers' biggest win of the campaign?
4. How many Premiership teams did Rangers beat in the 2014-15 season?
5. Which team did Rangers thrash 6-1 back in October, 2014?
6. Who did Rangers beat in their first match of 2015?
7. Who were Rangers' opponents for Stuart McCall's first game in charge?
8. Which two players – who both used to play in the capital – scored Rangers' goals in the vital 2-0 win over Hibs at Easter Road in March?
9. Which young player scored a double in the 3-1 win over Dumbarton in April?
10. Who scored Rangers' last goal of the season?

History Exam

**How well do you know your club's history?
See how you fare by answering these questions.**

1. In what year was the club founded?
2. How many times have Rangers played in a European final?
3. Who has made the most appearances for the club?
4. Who is the club's all-time top scorer?
5. Who has scored the most league goals for the club?
6. Who is the longest serving manager?
7. How many times have Rangers won the domestic treble?
8. How many of Rangers' "Greatest Ever Team" – as voted for by fans in 1999 – can you name?
9. Three of the club's players have been included in the Scottish Sports Hall of Fame – who are they?
10. Rangers played in front of their biggest crowd for a European match in September 1987 when 100,000 turned up to see them play a tie away from home. Who were the opponents?

Answers on page 61.

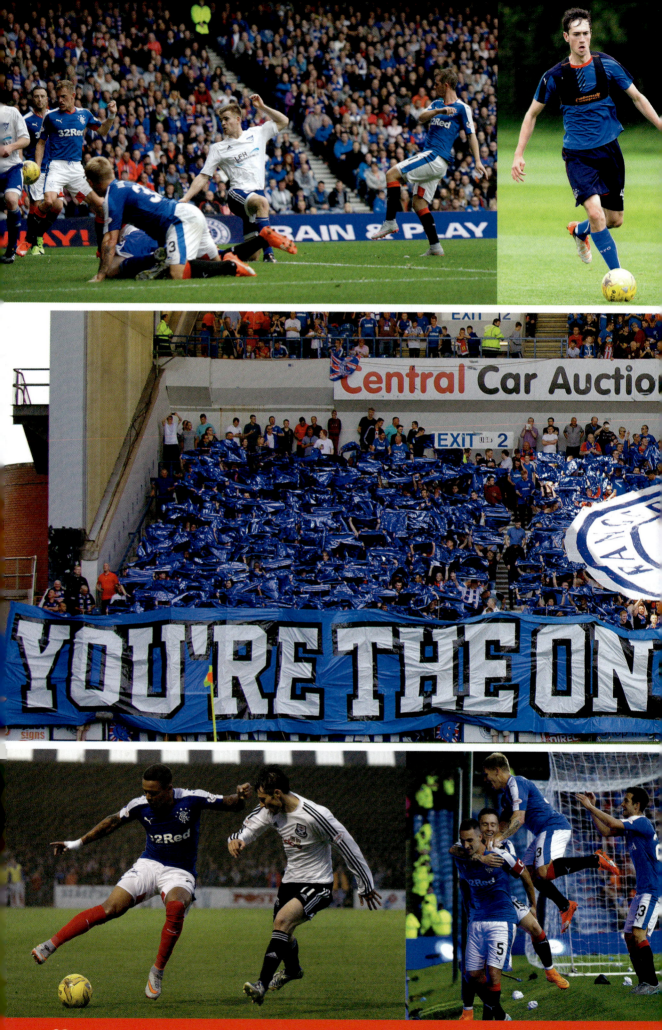

BUYING & SELLING OVER 1400 VEHICLES WEEKLY

WE

EXIT 3

TEAM FOR ME

THE BOSS

It is one of the most sought-after jobs in world football but it doesn't come without pressure. Here are some of the most successful managers in Rangers' history who have shown they can handle that pressure, and deliver silverware.

BILL STRUTH

Rangers' longest-serving and most successful manager. Struth was in the hot seat from 1920-54, winning 18 Scottish League titles, ten Scottish Cups and two League Cups.

In charge for 1,179 games, he had a winning percentage of 66.83. Struth set the benchmark in a different footballing era – how many managers today would be given over 34 years in charge?

SCOT SYMON

Had the difficult job of following in the footsteps of Struth, but was in charge for over 13 years (1954-67). He delivered six league titles, five Scottish Cups and four League Cups, averaging more than one trophy a year in his time at the helm.

He was in charge for almost 700 games and his winning percentage of 65.34 stands comparison with Struth.

WILLIE WADDELL

Willie Waddell was in charge for just over two-and-a-half years after arriving from Kilmarnock and has the distinction of guiding Rangers to their first European trophy.

Waddell's team of 1972 wrote themselves into Ibrox folklore with their memorable triumph in Barcelona, and ensured the manager was fondly remembered. His win percentage was 56.49.

JOCK WALLACE

Jock Wallace had two spells in charge at Ibrox, his initial spell from 1972-78 brought three Scottish League titles, three Scottish Cups and two League Cups and a winning percentage of 65.25.

He returned as manager in 1983 where he took charge for almost two-and-a-half years. But this time the league title proved elusive, although he did mastermind two League Cup triumphs. His winning percentage dropped to 43.65.

GRAEME SOUNESS

It is fair to say that Souness changed the face of Scottish football when he arrived as player-manager in April, 1986.

With the cheque-book open, Souness attracted the top players in Britain and beyond to Ibrox and it brought the club their first league title since the late 1970s. Souness delivered three Scottish League titles in all and four League Cups, but the Scottish Cup proved elusive. His winning percentage was 63.32.

WALTER SMITH

Walter Smith was the natural successor to Souness in 1991, having worked as assistant manager under the former Scotland international.

Like Wallace, he had two spells in charge and is the only manager to come close to Struth in terms of silverware, although there is no doubt Smith achieved his success in a more competitive era.

In his first spell as manager (1991-98), Smith won seven league titles, three Scottish Cups and one League Cup (winning percentage 65.52) and, in his second stint (2007-11), he won three league titles, two Scottish Cups and three League Cups as well as taking Rangers to a European final (winning percentage 62.86).

DICK ADVOCAAT

The highly-respected Dutchman was a bold choice to follow Smith's first spell as Rangers' manager and he went on to record the best winning percentage of any boss in the top flight at 67.53.

Advocaat was at the helm for three-and-a-half years (1998-01), almost 200 matches in total, and won two league titles, two Scottish Cups and one League Cup.

ALEX MCLEISH

McLeish was a surprise appointment to follow Advocaat after cutting his managerial teeth at Motherwell and Hibs. He spent almost four-and-a-half years in charge and delivered two league championship titles, two Scottish Cups and three League Cups.

His winning percentage of 65.96 stands in comparison with the best.

SEE IF YOU CAN WORK OUT WHO THESE PAST AND PRESENT RANGERS STARS ARE FROM THE CLUES PROVIDED.

1
a) I am a striker and I signed for the club three times.
b) I have played football in Scotland, England, Turkey and Canada.
c) I have been capped for Scotland on 69 occasions.

2
a) I started my career at Cowdenbeath and helped them win the third division in 2006.
b) I had a spell in junior football with Arniston Rangers.
c) Before joining Rangers, I played for St Mirren.

3
a) I started my career at Burnley but joined Everton in a £300,000 deal when I was 19.
b) I went on to win 36 caps for England.
c) I won a European Cup-Winners' Cup medal and scored in the final – but not with Rangers!

4
a) I started my career with Armadale Thistle.
b) I had two spells at Rangers and also played for Coventry City.
c) I once scored four goals in an international game for Scotland.

5
a) I made my Rangers debut in August 2013 against East Fife.
b) My dad also played for the club.
c) I scored 41 goals in my final season at Queen of the South.

6
a) I had two spells at Ibrox but also signed for Hearts twice.
b) I was a member of the Rangers treble-winning team in 1992-93.
c) I had a brief spell as player-manager at Morton.

7
a) I was born in the Netherlands and signed for Rangers from FC Twente.
b) I won five league titles at Ibrox but left to play in Japan.
c) I am now a coach and have had spells at Ajax, Groningen and the Indonesian national team.

8
a) I signed for Rangers for a then British record fee of £4 million.
b) I only had a short time at Ibrox but it is fair to say it was eventful.
c) I won an FA Cup winners' medal with Everton in 1995.

9
a) I was born in Germany and signed for Rangers in 1968.
b) I won a League Cup winners' medal in 1970, helping the team beat Celtic in the final.
c) My daughter was an international athlete for Scotland.

10
a) I was born in Spain and joined Rangers after playing for another two Scottish clubs.
b) I scored 25 goals in my first season at the club.
c) I demonstrated a cool head by scoring the winner in the penalty shoot-out at Fiorentina in the semi-final of the UEFA Cup in 2008.

WHO AM I

(Answers on page 61)

Can you find 19 famous Rangers names in the jumble of letters? You can go horizontally, vertically, diagonally and backwards.

```
N E T T O T Y J W C T D M L Y
M J X J H J Z R J K U N N L C
T A A C O V D A H R O O O A W
T D M P T K W S R T F M T C R
M S H N B K I A R H S Y N C R
C D I D O E N U L S W S R M S
D C F O L T B Q E E N L O Q T
O B C C C R L N W L G P H M R
W R M M A C U I W A R U T M U
A Y Y W G O M H W H L Y E H T
L V T X S Q I W F R M L Q N H
L N L Z R T R L L Q Z X A Z M
W A D D E L L R X L N R H C C
G R T S M I T H R X K Z Y F E
T R Z T Q Z P N N N A E L C M
```

Advocaat	**McCoist**	**Smith**	**Thornton**	**Warburton**
Durrant	**McDowall**	**Souness**	**Totten**	**White**
LeGuen	**McLean**	**Struth**	**Waddell**	**Wilton**
McCall	**McLeish**	**Symon**	**Wallace**	

TIMELINE

1872 Club founded.

1877 Club reaches its first Scottish Cup final.

1878 First trophy won – the Glasgow Merchants' Charity Cup.

1888 First Old Firm game.

1890 Formation of Scottish League, Rangers is one of ten original member teams.

1891 Club's first league title – shared with Dumbarton.

1894 Club's first Scottish Cup triumph, beating Celtic 3-1 in final.

1899 Rangers win league with 100 per cent record. Ibrox Park opened.

1902 First Ibrox Disaster – 25 fans killed and 517 injured after collapse of terracing.

1920 Bill Struth – who became Rangers' most successful manager – appointed to succeed William Wilton.

1939 A British League record attendance of 118,567 watched the New Year fixture with Celtic.

1948 Club plays in front of its biggest crowd when 143,570 watch Scottish Cup semi-final with Hibs at Hampden.

1949 Rangers win the domestic treble for first time.

1954 Scot Symon took over as manager to lead a new era.

1960 Club reaches the semi-finals of the European Cup, losing to Germans Eintracht Frankfurt.

1961 First British club to reach a European final, but lost 4-1 on aggregate to Italians Fiorentina in Cup-Winners' Cup.

1964 Rangers win the domestic treble for the second time.

1967 Reach final of European Cup-Winners' Cup for second time, but lose 1-0 to Bayern Munich in extra-time.

Top row: G. Gillespie, W. McNeil, P. Campbell, J. Watt
Middle row: W. Dunlop, D. Hill, T. Vallance, S. Ricketts, M. McNeil
Front row: J. Watson, A Marshall

1971 Second Ibrox Disaster – 66 fans lose their lives at the end of Old Firm game on New Year's Day.

1972 Rangers win a European trophy – beating Moscow Dynamo 3-2 – in Cup-Winners' Cup final in Barcelona.

1975 Club wins the Scottish League for the first time in 11 years under Jock Wallace's stewardship.

1976 Rangers win the domestic treble.

1978 Rangers win another treble.

1986 Graeme Souness takes over as manager.

1989 Rangers win first league title under Souness.

1993 Fifth domestic treble.

1997 Club wins its ninth successive title – the first three under Souness, the last six under Walter Smith. Home ground renamed Ibrox Stadium.

1998 Dick Advocaat becomes the club's first foreign manager.

1999 Advocaat guides team to their sixth domestic treble.

2001 Murray Park is opened as the club's training ground.

2003 Alex McLeish is in charge as Rangers win their seventh treble, including a world record 50th league title.

2005 "Helicopter Sunday" as Rangers snatch the league title on the last day of the season from Celtic at Easter Road.

2008 Walter Smith, in his second spell in charge, guides Rangers to the UEFA Cup final.

2012 Rangers placed into administration.

2015 Dave King gains control, and Mark Warburton and David Weir are appointed as the new management team.

THE SIGNIFICANT DATES IN RANGERS' HISTORY

THE MAKING OF MARK

Mark was brought up in London and showed at school that he was a promising footballer.

The defender started out as an apprentice under former Scotland defender Frank McLintock at Leicester City, but parted company with the club after Jock Wallace took over as manager.

He had a successful four years playing non-league football with Enfield Town, winning the FA Trophy in 1981-82 and the Alliance Premier League the following season.

Mark then joined Isthmian League side Boreham Wood and played over 100 games for them before a spell playing in America, in Charlotte and Chicago, while he was working in finance.

He had to give up playing after cruciate ligament damage, and started coaching at St Clement Danes School in Chorley Wood before working as a city trader in London.

Mark spent time travelling around Europe studying the coaching methods of Barcelona, Sporting Lisbon and Ajax, amongst others, as he sought to gain a foothold in the professional game.

Mark Warburton arrived at Ibrox last summer after a unique background finally brought him one of the top coaching jobs in European football. Here, we plot his rise to the top.

He was used to working long hours in his career – as a city trader, he left his house before 5am and did not return until 7pm on a daily basis.

His big break in coaching came when he was taken on by Watford full-time to look after their academy programme, from Under-Nine to Under-16 level, and was made manager of their academy in 2006, leaving the club in February 2010.

Mark was appointed first-team coach at Brentford a year later, before moving on to become sporting director a few months later, a new position that meant dealing with players' contracts.

He was given the manager's job in December 2013, appointing Davie Weir as his assistant within a week. The team won six games in a row and Mark was named League One Manager of the Month.

Brentford put together 19 league matches without defeat until Wolves punctured the remarkable record with a 3-0 away win.

The club was promoted to the Championship after a 1-0 win against Preston North End in April 2014, finishing the season as runners-up to Wolves. In 27 games in charge, Mark had only lost four.

Mark once took some of his players to the dealing floor at HSBC to show them the kinds of pressures city traders worked under.

He continued to make his mark in the Championship where he established a new club record of five successive wins in the second tier of English football. But it was revealed by club owner Matthew Benham that the manager's contract would not be renewed at the end of the 2014-15 season due to internal restructuring.

Mark guided Brentford to a lofty fifth place in the table and into the play-offs where they lost in the semi-finals 5-1 on aggregate to Middlesbrough.

His overall record in charge at Brentford was the best in the club's history – winning 40 of his 78 matches, drawing 16 and losing 22.

He used just 24 players during the 2014-15 season, the joint-fewest in the division.

Mark's son, Jack, has represented Northern Ireland at Under-16 and Under-17 level.

He was one of the founders of the NextGen Series – a European club cup competition for Under-19 teams set up in 2011. But lack of funding meant that the 2013-14 competition was cancelled.

Mark was linked to jobs at Fulham and Derby County before he put pen to paper on a three-year deal at Ibrox last June.

TREBLE YELL

Rangers have won the domestic treble for a World Record seven times. Here, we dig into history and celebrate the years where the club ruled all they surveyed in domestic football. There is also an in-depth look at the last treble under Alex McLeish in 2002-03.

1948-49 (MANAGER: BILL STRUTH)

LEAGUE CUP

Rangers won the inaugural competition in 1946-47 and reclaimed the trophy on the first leg of the treble. In those days, the competition was initially played in sectional qualifying rounds and Rangers opened with two draws – 1-1 v Clyde at Ibrox and 0-0 v Hibs at Easter Road – before losing 3-1 to Celtic at Parkhead.

But Rangers reached the last eight by winning the return matches (3-1 v Clyde, 1-0 v Hibs and 3-1 v Celtic) and beat St Mirren 1-0 in the quarter-finals. Dundee were beaten 4-1 in the semi-finals and Rangers hoisted the silverware by beating Raith Rovers 2-0 in the final, with goals from Torrance Gillick and Willie Paton.

SCOTTISH CUP

Rangers blew away the opposition on the way to their Scottish Cup triumph. The tone was set with a 6-1 dismissal of Elgin City in the first round on a cold January day at Ibrox. Rangers did not concede another goal en route to the final, beating Motherwell 3-0, Partick Thistle 4-0 and then East Fife 3-0 in the semi-finals. In front of 120,162 fans in the Hampden final, Rangers saw off Clyde 4-1, with George Young scoring two penalty kicks and Billy Williamson and Jimmy Duncanson also on target.

LEAGUE

Rangers completed the domestic treble by securing the league championship a week after their cup success, beating Albion Rovers 4-1 away from home. Willie Thornton scored a hat-trick and Jimmy Duncanson was also on target as Rangers pipped Dundee by just a point to take the title.

The team opened with a 1-1 draw against Motherwell at Fir Park (Thornton scored the goal) and drew three of their first five matches. Thornton finished top league scorer with 23 goals but it was a team effort and many of the names from that treble-winning side are part of Rangers' folklore – Thornton, Willie Woodburn, Ian McColl, Willie Waddell, Sammy Cox, Jock Shaw and Bobby Brown amongst them.

1963-64 (MANAGER: SCOTT SYMON)

LEAGUE CUP

Rangers eased through their qualifying section, only a 2-2 draw with Kilmarnock in their final match at Ibrox denying them a 100 per cent record. The free-scoring team scored 22 goals in six qualifying matches, beating Celtic 3-0 home and away, twice easing past Queen of the South 5-2 and beating Kilmarnock 4-1 at Rugby Park.

It set up a two-leg quarter-final with East Fife; Rangers drawing 1-1 away before winning 2-0 at Ibrox. Berwick Rangers were brushed aside 3-1 in the semi-finals and the final, against Morton in front of 105,907 fans at Hampden, was even easier as Jim Forrest netted four times and Alex Willoughby once in a 5-0 victory.

SCOTTISH CUP

Rangers started out on the cup trail with a 5-1 win over Stenhousemuir in the first round. They then thumped non-league Duns 9-0 in the second round and Partick Thistle 3-0 to reach the last eight. Rangers beat Celtic 2-0 and then Dunfermline 1-0 in the semi-final to face a strong Dundee team in the final that included Bobby Cox, Andy Penman and Alan Gilzean. Hampden Park was again packed, with 120,982 seeing Rangers win 3-1 with Jimmy Millar (2) and Ralph Brand getting the goals.

LEAGUE

Rangers won the title with room to spare, losing just four of their 34 games. It was a powerful Rangers team that included Bobby Shearer, John Greig, Ron McKinnon, Jim Baxter, Willie Henderson and Ralph Brand so there was power and panache throughout the side. Rangers finished the season with a six-point cushion on second-placed Kilmarnock with Celtic and Hearts a further two points adrift.

1975-76 (MANAGER: JOCK WALLACE)

LEAGUE CUP

Rangers opened with a 6-1 win over Airdrie at Ibrox with Sandy Jardine unusually scoring a hat-trick, two of his goals from the penalty spot. Clyde (1-0, 6-0), Motherwell (1-1, 2-2) and a 2-1 win over Airdrie at

Broomfield ensured Rangers qualified for a two-leg quarter-final against Queen of the South, where the team won 1-0 at home and drew 2-2 at Palmerston Park. Montrose were put to the sword 5-1 in the semi-finals and Rangers took the first silverware of the season by beating Celtic 1-0 in the final, Alex MacDonald heading the only goal.

LEAGUE

Rangers wrapped up the title in their third-last game of the season when a goal from

Derek Johnstone inside the first 30 seconds was enough for a 1-0 win over Dundee United at Tannadice. Rangers opened the season with a 2-1 victory over Celtic and opened the defence of their title with three successive wins. But Jock Wallace's side struggled after that and won just one of their next seven games. But it all turned out fine as they won 16 of their final 21 games and finished the season with a six-point cushion over closest challengers Celtic.

SCOTTISH CUP

Rangers completed the treble by beating Hearts 3-1 at Hampden in front of 85,354 fans. Derek Johnstone scored twice and Alex MacDonald also found the net in what turned out to be a comfortable victory. Johnstone, the club's top scorer, netted in every round apart from the third round as Rangers defeated East Fife 3-0. The team progressed to the quarter-finals with a handsome 4-1 win over Aberdeen, then beat Queen of the South 5-0, Johnstone scoring twice. Johnstone also scored a double in the narrow 3-2 semi-final win over Motherwell.

1977-78 (MANAGER: JOCK WALLACE)

LEAGUE CUP

The format of the competition had changed with no sectional qualifiers and a straight knock-out contest, albeit with home-and-away ties up until the semi-final stage. Rangers saw off St Johnstone 3-1 and 3-0, then Aberdeen 6-1 and 1-3, and Dunfermline 3-1 and 3-1. Rangers beat plucky Forfar 5-2 in the semi-finals to set up another Old Firm final, Rangers beating Celtic 2-1 after extra-time with goals from Davie Cooper and Gordon Smith.

LEAGUE

Rangers had recruited Cooper, Smith and Bobby Russell during the summer but the league campaign did not start off well with successive defeats to Aberdeen and Hibs. But there was a pivotal 3-2 win over Celtic early in the season after trailing 2-0. An emergent Aberdeen won 3-0 at Ibrox to put pressure on the leaders, but Rangers finished the campaign in style by winning their final four matches without losing a goal to take the title by just two points ahead of Aberdeen.

SCOTTISH CUP

Jock Wallace became the first (and, so far, only) manager to guide Rangers to two trebles as he guided the team to the Scottish Cup. Any nerves about drawing Berwick Rangers in the third round at Shielfield Park after 1967 were dispelled as Rangers won 4-2. Stirling Albion (1-0) and Kilmarnock (4-1) were also erased from the competition and Rangers reached another final with a 2-0 victory over Dundee United. Alex MacDonald and Derek Johnstone were on target as Rangers beat Aberdeen 2-1 in the final.

1992-93 (MANAGER: WALTER SMITH)

LEAGUE CUP

Rangers opened with an impressive 5-0 win over Dumbarton in the second round and repeated the scoreline against Stranraer in round three. Dundee United provided more of a challenge in the quarter-finals, Rangers winning 3-2, and the club reached another final by beating St Johnstone 3-1 in the semi-finals. In a tight final with Aberdeen that required extra-time, Rangers won through 2-1 with goals from Stuart McCall and an own goal from Gary Smith.

LEAGUE

Rangers swept to their fifth successive league title in a momentous season that saw Walter Smith's side reach the brink of the inaugural Champions League. Rangers played 64 matches in total in a busy campaign but they kept their focus throughout. A 4-3 loss to Dundee in August did no harm as it wasn't until the following March that the team lost another league game (2-1 to Celtic). Ally McCoist finished top scorer in the league with 34 goals, and was to score 49 in all competitions. Rangers finished nine points ahead of second-placed Aberdeen.

SCOTTISH CUP

Rangers won the Scottish Cup "on the road" as they completed the treble in spite of the fact that none of their ties were at Ibrox. Motherwell were beaten 2-0 in the third round at Fir Park, before Rangers travelled to Somerset Park in the fourth round to face Ayr United, also winning 2-0. Then it was off to Arbroath in the quarter-finals – Rangers winning 3-0 – before edging Hearts 2-1 in the semi-final. Goals from Neil Murray and Mark Hateley gave Rangers silverware, with another 2-1 final win over Aberdeen after extra-time.

1998-99 (MANAGER: DICK ADVOCAAT)

LEAGUE CUP

Dick Advocaat won his first silverware within a few months of taking charge after watching over a major change in player personnel over the summer. Rangers only lost one goal on the way to the trophy and that was in the final, winning 2-1 against St Johnstone with Stephane Guivarc'h and Jorg Albertz contributing the goals. Alloa Athletic (4-0), Ayr United (2-0) and Airdrie (5-0) were all put to the sword in previous rounds.

LEAGUE

With much anticipation in the air Rangers lost their league opener 2-1 to Hearts, but it did not take long for the new-look team to get into their stride. Advocaat's team did not taste defeat again in the league until late October (to Motherwell) and their class was evident throughout the season as they punctuated it with some crushing wins (7-0 v St Johnstone, 6-1 v Dundee, 5-0 v Kilmarnock). Rangers clinched the title with a 3-0 win at Celtic Park in an emotive contest and finished the season six points clear of their oldest rivals. Rod Wallace was top league scorer with 19 goals.

SCOTTISH CUP

Rangers completed the treble by beating Celtic 1-0 in the cup final at Hampden, Rod Wallace scoring the goal early in the second half. The team beat Stenhousemuir 2-0 in the third round and then won 6-0 at Hamilton Academical in round four. Falkirk were beaten 2-1 in the quarter-finals – the only goal Rangers conceded on the way to the trophy – and there was a resounding 4-0 win over St Johnstone in the semi-final at Celtic Park. Advocaat had scooped all of the domestic honours in his first season.

2002-03 (MANAGER: ALEX MCLEISH)

LEAGUE CUP

Rangers took care of Hibs 3-2 at Easter Road in the third round. Ian Murray put the home side in front but Rangers equalised through an own goal from Derek Townsley in 22 minutes. Three minutes later, Caniggia put Rangers in front but Garry O'Connor equalised in 72 minutes. Lovenkrands made it 3-2 six minutes later, and Hibs finished short-handed with Gary Smith sent off for a second bookable offence.

Caniggia was on target again in the quarter-finals as Rangers beat Dunfermline 1-0 at East End Park through his 79th-minute strike.

There was only one goal in the semi-final against Hearts as Rangers claimed the second half of a capital double with a 1-0 win thanks to de Boer's first-half goal.

It set up an Old Firm final and Rangers had established a 2-0 lead at half-time through Caniggia and Lovenkrands. Larsson pulled a goal back for Celtic early in the second half, but Rangers triumphed 2-1 with Neil Lennon sent off two minutes from time for Celtic. The first trophy was in the cabinet.

LEAGUE CHAMPIONSHIP

It started out at Rugby Park. Shota Arveladze scored Rangers' first league goal of the campaign, but Kilmarnock hit back to earn a 1-1 draw with a late Andy McLaren goal.

Rangers then reeled off eight successive league wins – including a 6-0 demolition of Dunfermline – and the only team to score against them in those matches was Hibs (who Rangers beat 4-2).

It set it up nicely for the first Old Firm clash of the season at Celtic Park in October. It was to be a classic confrontation – Mikel Arteta gave Rangers an early lead, only for Celtic to hit back with a Henrik Larsson double. Ronald de Boer equalised and Arveladze put Rangers back in front, only for Chris Sutton to equalise with 12 minutes left in a breathless 3-3 draw.

Rangers went on to win ten of their next 11 matches – only a 2-2 draw with Aberdeen at Pittodrie ruining their record and including a 3-2 win over Celtic at Ibrox – before the first league defeat of the season arrived, in a Boxing Day clash at Motherwell with James McFadden scoring the only goal.

Rangers responded in the best possible way – seven successive wins before Celtic burst the bubble with a 1-0 win at Celtic Park courtesy of John Hartson.

Into the final furlong, and it could hardly be more dramatic. Celtic won 2-1 at Ibrox with goals from Alan Thompson and Hartson in the first half before de Boer replied and it was Rangers' only defeat in the final eight matches.

But two precious points were dropped in a 2-2 draw with Dundee and it took a late penalty from Arteta to salvage that. And so it went down to the final day of the season with Rangers and Celtic on the same number of points.

McLeish's men rose to the occasion to beat Dunfermline 6-1 and clinch the title on goal difference – by just one goal! Michael Mols, Claudio Caniggia, Arveladze, de Boer, Steven Thompson and Arteta all found the net at Ibrox to spark the celebrations. Trophy number two was secured.

SCOTTISH CUP

Rangers were drawn away at Arbroath in the third round and came through comfortably enough 3-0 with goals from Barry Ferguson, Craig Moore and Arveladze. It brought a tricky fourth round tie at Somerset Park but Rangers booked their quarter-final place with a goal from de Boer with just 12 minutes left.

Rangers faced Dunfermline at East End Park in the quarter-finals and it was the home side who took the lead midway through the first half, David Grondin netting. Caniggia equalised within eight minutes as the game finished 1-1, but Rangers finished with ten men after a red card for Ferguson.

Rangers made no mistake in the replay at Ibrox, winning 3-0 with Peter Lovenkrands, Ferguson and Arteta all finding the net.

The semi-final with Motherwell was a seven-goal thriller – Rangers scoring early through Bert Konterman but finding themselves behind at half-time as the Fir Park side hit back through Steven Craig and McFadden. Michael Mols, Lorenzo Amoruso and an own goal from David Partridge put Rangers 4-2 in control before Motherwell scored a last-minute consolation through Derek Adams as it finished 4-3.

Dundee provided the final opponents and it was a tight match, with Rangers taking the silverware 1-0 through an Amoruso strike midway through the second half. The treble was assured.

Euro Nights

Ibrox has rocked to some rousing nights in Europe. Here, we look back on five of the best to whet the appetite for more to follow.

EUROPEAN CUP-WINNERS' CUP:
SEMI-FINAL, SECOND LEG, APRIL 19, 1972:
RANGERS 2 BAYERN MUNICH 0

Rangers humbled one of the greatest club teams in European history to reach the 1972 final.

Ibrox was packed to capacity to see if Rangers could go through after drawing the first leg 1-1 in Munich.

Bayern had a formidable squad at the time, including Sepp Maier, Franz Beckenbauer, Paul Breitner, Uli Hoeness and Gerd Müller, mainstays of the German team that won the World Cup two years later.

Rangers were without the injured John Greig, but Sandy Jardine set the tone by scoring from long range early on. Derek Parlane clinched a place in the final with the decisive second goal.

Souvenir Special
Wednesday 19th April, 1972 Price: 5p

22578

RANGERS

EUROPEAN CUP WINNERS TROPHY

1971·72 SEMI FINALS 2ND LEG

versus BAYERN

CHAMPIONS LEAGUE –
SECOND ROUND, FIRST LEG:
OCTOBER 21, 1992:

RANGERS 2 LEEDS UNITED 1

The long-awaited "Battle of Britain" lived up to expectations as a crowd of 43,251 packed Ibrox. The English champions were strong favourites going into the two-leg tie to decide who would become Britain's first representative in the group stage of the restructured competition. Leeds included Gordon Strachan, Eric Cantona and David Batty, and Gary McAllister silenced Ibrox in the second minute with a volley after Strachan's

corner. Rangers equalised midway through the first half when John Lukic punched the ball into his own net from a corner. Ally McCoist netted what proved to be the winner four minutes from half-time when he pounced after the goalkeeper had saved Dave McPherson's header. Rangers also won the return 2-1 at Elland Road.

CHAMPIONS LEAGUE – GROUP STAGE:
NOVEMBER 25, 1992:
RANGERS 2 MARSEILLE 2

Rangers produced one of the greatest European comebacks to take a valuable point in the revamped Champions League.

The French champions included Fabien Barthez, Basile Boli, Franck Sauzee, Marcel Desailly and Didier Deschamps in a star-studded line-up.

Alen Boksic gave them the lead in the 31st minute and German striker Rudi Völler made it 2-0 ten minutes after the break.

With time running out, Gary McSwegan replaced Trevor Steven after 75 minutes and within a minute had pulled a goal back.

Mark Hateley then equalised with eight minutes left as Ibrox went wild.

OCTOBER 27, 2007:

RANGERS 0 BARCELONA 0

Rangers produced a supreme defensive display to frustrate the Spanish giants and gain a valuable and unexpected Champions League point.

Walter Smith produced a masterful tactical plan as Rangers matched one of the great Barcelona teams that included Carles Puyol, Lilian Thuram, Andres Iniesta, Xavi, Ronaldinho, Thierry Henry and Lionel Messi.

Allan McGregor produced a string of superb saves and Henry missed the target with an easy header in the second half.

Rangers could even have won it in the closing stages – Nacho Novo and Barry Ferguson both failed to get on the end of a Daniel Cousin cross before Cousin fired over from an angle.

RANGERS
FIORENTINA

0
0 (90)

UEFA CUP – SEMI-FINAL, FIRST LEG:

APRIL 24, 2008:

RANGERS 0 FIORENTINA 0

Rangers took an important step towards the UEFA Cup final with a disciplined display against Italian cracks Fiorentina.

In a season where Rangers saved their best form for their European travels, it was key not to give up a goal at Ibrox.

Fiorentina had long spells of possession but Neil Alexander was not over-worked in the Rangers goal.

He saved early on from Martin Jorgensen, and Adrian Mutu tested him late on, but it was another victory for Walter Smith's tactics.

Nacho Novo came close with an ambitious long-range effort as Rangers also had their chances.

But it was a supreme defensive display, with Carlos Cuellar having an outstanding game for the home side.

Fiorentina sent on Christian Vieri in the closing stages but he could not unlock the Rangers' defence.

Rangers completed the job in Florence, Novo scoring the winning goal in a penalty shoot-out after another 0-0 draw.

QUIZ ANSWERS

WORDSEARCH (PAGE 36)

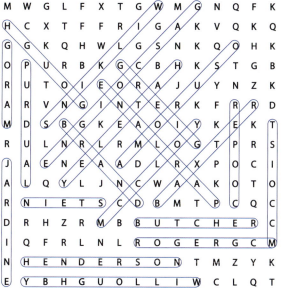

HISTORY EXAM (PAGE 37)

1 1872
2 Four – the European Cup-Winners' Cup in 1961, 1967 and 1972 and the UEFA Cup in 2008
3 John Greig – 755 between 1960-78
4 Ally McCoist – 355 goals from 1983-98
5 Ally McCoist – 251
6 Bill Struth was in charge for 34 years and 26 days
7 Seven – 1948-49, 1963-64, 1975-76, 1977-78, 1992-93, 1998-99, 2002-03
8 The team was: Andy Goram, Sandy Jardine, Richard Gough, Terry Butcher, John Greig, Brian Laudrup, Paul Gascoigne, Jim Baxter, Davie Cooper, Ally McCoist and Mark Hateley
9 Jim Baxter, John Greig and Ally McCoist
10 Dynamo Kiev

WORDSEARCH (PAGE 45)

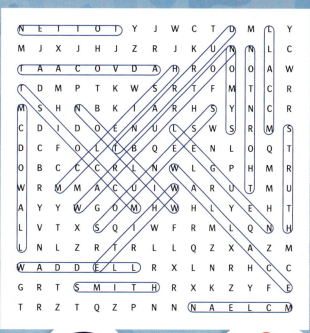

QUIZ (PAGE 37)

2014-15 Quiz

1 Lewis Macleod (v Hibs in the Petrofac Training Cup)
2 Nicky Law (v Hearts)
3 8-1 (v Clyde in the Petrofac Training Cup)
4 Three – Inverness Caledonian Thistle, St Johnstone and Kilmarnock
5 Raith Rovers
6 Dumbarton (3-1 at Ibrox)
7 Livingston – the match finished 1-1 in March
8 Lee Wallace and Kenny Miller
9 Ryan Hardie
10 Darren McGregor

WHO AM I? (PAGE 44)

1 Kenny Miller
2 Darren McGregor
3 Trevor Steven
4 Colin Stein
5 Nicky Clark
6 Dave McPherson
7 Peter Huistra
8 Duncan Ferguson
9 Gerry Neef
10 Nacho Novo